MW00698987

TEN
PRINCIPLES
FOR BIBLICAL
LIVING

Don Sisk

Ps 126:5,6

DON SISK

Copyright © 2006 by Striving Together Publications. All
Scripture quotations are taken from
the King James Version.

First published in 2006 by Striving Together Publications, a
ministry of Lancaster Baptist Church, Lancaster, CA 93535.
Striving Together Publications is committed to providing
tried, trusted, and proven books that will further equip
local churches to carry out the Great Commission. Your
comments and suggestions are valued.

All rights reserved. No part of this book may be
reproduced, stored in a retrieval system, or transmitted
in any form or by any means—electronic, mechanical,
photocopy, recording, or otherwise—without written
permission of the publisher, except for brief quotations in
printed reviews.

Striving Together Publications
4020 E. Lancaster Blvd.
Lancaster, CA 93535
800.201.7748

Edited by Michelle Gardner,
Agnes Huffmaster, and Cary Schmidt
Cover design by Jeremy Lofgren
Layout by Jeremy Lofgren and Craig Parker

ISBN 1-59894-009-0

Printed in the United States of America

DEDICATION

I would like to dedicate this book to Dr. Ray Thompson. Virginia and I met Dr. and Mrs. Thompson the day we were accepted by BIMI as missionaries to Japan. They also joined BIMI on that day. Since that day in June of 1964, the Thompsons have been our good friends. For many years we rarely saw each other. When they returned to Chattanooga to assume the position of Caribbean Director and we returned to be the Far Eastern Director, we worked very closely together and our friendship grew. In 1983, when I was asked to be the General Director of BIMI, I requested of the board that they appoint Dr. Thompson as my assistant.

For nearly twenty years, we worked hand and heart together in those positions. I could not ask for a more faithful, knowledgeable and proficient fellow laborer. He has been greatly used of God in worldwide evangelism for over fifty years. Only eternity will tell the results of the labor of this great man of God. It gives me much pleasure to dedicate this book to him.

TABLE OF CONTENTS

FOREWORD

From Dr. Paul Chappell,
Pastor of Lancaster Baptist Church and
President of West Coast Baptist College

Dear Friend,

Dr. Don Sisk is not only a great man of God, he is a dear friend. He has been a faithful servant of Jesus Christ for nearly six decades; he loves his wife and his family faithfully; and God has greatly used him for the cause of Christ around the world.

In spite of God's great blessings upon his ministry, Dr. Sisk is one of the most sincere and humble men of God I have ever met. He is a truly joyful Christian who loves serving God and loves reaching people for Christ. His influence upon modern day world missions is profound, and his spirit is uniquely Christ-like.

Some time ago, I heard Dr. Sisk present these ten principles, and now I am delighted to see them placed into this powerful book. I know God will greatly encourage your life as you read and apply these biblical truths.

May God bless you as you read!

Sincerely,

Pastor Paul Chappell
Lancaster, California

INTRODUCTION

We live in a world that is completely alienated from God. Most people have no direction or purpose for living. Life is just happening to them, seemingly by default. Many are misled into thinking success equals a big number—how many cars you own, how much money you make, how much you have in the bank, or how much your house is worth. Like a ship without a rudder, they flounder through life, mindless of the fact that there is a God who loves them and has a wonderful plan and purpose for their lives.

If you know Jesus Christ as your Saviour, then you have a purpose for living. Salvation is simply the first step of a wonderful life-journey of commitment and faithfulness to Jesus Christ. Staying faithful to Christ, keeping a good spirit, and finishing the race are challenges that every

Christian faces and battles that every Christian can win, if they depend on the principles and power of the Word of God.

In my Christian walk and ministry, I have often been reminded that I need help! Life throws a lot of unexpected challenges. The road doesn't always lead where we think it will. We need guideposts along the way to help us stay faithful and committed to the cause of Christ. Thank God, Jesus is our Navigator, and His Word is our compass. Though we can't always see where life will take us, we can rest in confidence that He knows the way, and we can trust the principles of His Word to guide us day by day.

Psalm 119:105 says, "*Thy word is a lamp unto my feet, and a light unto my path.*" The question is, how do we appropriate His truths and precepts into our lives? Is it really possible to live according to what we believe? How do we uphold the doctrines of the Bible within the framework of our lives?

Throughout my Christian journey, the Lord has taught me many valuable lessons that have enabled me, not only to get through problems and trials, but also to stay in the race with a joyful spirit. Some time ago, I began to articulate the guiding principles that have been foundational in my life and ministry. After much prayer and thought, I defined ten guiding principles that I believe God has blessed over these many years. I felt compelled to begin teaching these principles, first to our missionaries and staff at Baptist International Missions, Inc., then to

Christian leaders and Bible college students from all over the country. Now, I pray they will encourage your life as you read them from the pages of this book.

These pages explain the principles that, to this day, have helped me make right decisions based on the Word of God. A principle is defined as "a personal or specific basis of conduct; an accepted or professed rule of action." When biblical principles guide our lives, we can avoid making decisions based on whim or emotion. Principles help us predetermine what we will do when temptation or discouragement comes. It's easy to fall into the trap of making poor choices because of how we feel or because of the immediate circumstances we face, rather than based upon the unchanging truth of the Word of God. In Psalm 119:9 the psalmist says, "*Wherewithal shall a young man cleanse his way? by taking heed thereto according to thy word.*"

Each of these principles is founded upon Scripture and leads us to submit to God's Word for our everyday decisions. Looking back on fifty-two years of ministry, I can honestly say that God has blessed these guidelines in my life. I do not regret living my life by the Word of God and for the glory of God. His Word has never failed!

One of the principles my wife, Virginia, and I have lived by has to do with debt. Many years ago, we committed that we would not take on any debt other than a house or an automobile. Applying this particular principle in our lives has enabled us to obey the Lord whenever and wherever

He wanted us to go. Debt is often a hindrance that keeps people from obeying God's call or leading in their lives. In Romans 13:8 Paul admonishes to "*owe no man any thing.*"

This principle brought about a set course of action— a predetermined response for times we would want something that we couldn't afford. We never went into debt for groceries, vacation, or some possession that didn't have legitimate equity value.

David writes in Psalm 37:25, "*I have been young, and now am old; yet have I not seen the righteous forsaken, nor his seed begging bread.*" God has always provided for our every need! He has honored our obedience to His biblical principles.

Dr. Lee Roberson, the great man of God who pastored Highland Park Baptist Church for more than forty years, decided that other than his family members, he would never be alone in the presence of a lady. As he pastored, there was glass in his office door and there were people outside his office at all times. He would not be in a car or a room alone with a member of the opposite sex. Dr. Roberson saw the importance of 1 Thessalonians 5:22, which says, "*Abstain from all appearance of evil.*" He let this Scripture provide a principle by which he lived his life faithfully for many years in the ministry.

The Apostle Paul led a truly amazing life. From the time of his conversion to the end of his life, he never got tired of doing what the Lord had called him to do. Although he experienced many difficulties and many trials, he regarded the ministry as a great privilege. I believe that Paul became the man God wanted him to be, because he appropriated biblical principles into his life. He learned to be content. He learned to be joyful in the face of extreme hardship. He learned to be steadfast despite persecution. Near the end of his life, he wrote these words in 1 Timothy 1:12, "*And I thank Christ Jesus our Lord, who hath enabled me, for that he counted me faithful, putting me into the ministry.*"

It is only by His grace that I am still in the ministry after fifty-two wonderful years. I have had the privilege of serving the Lord with my wife and children as missionaries to Japan. God has allowed me, through Baptist International Missions, Inc., to preach in over thirteen hundred missions conferences, in one thousand churches, and in sixty-five countries. For over thirty years I have traveled to different places every week. I sometimes tell people that I feel like a drug addict because I'm always on a trip!

What a blessing it is to simply stay faithful to Jesus Christ! What a blessing it is to be a recipient of God's infinite grace! We who serve the Lord Jesus Christ ought to be thankful that He allows us to do so! Truly, ministry is a privilege that we ought to never get over!

I have cherished every moment of knowing Jesus as my Lord and Saviour for fifty-six years. I have been a preacher for fifty-one rewarding years, and I have never grown tired of serving God! Every morning His mercies are new, and every day His strength guides and blesses our lives. How wonderfully and wondrously God has provided for me and for my family!

It is my prayer that these biblical principles will be a blessing to you as you apply them to your life. I trust that many years from now, you will look back to the time when you made the decision to live by these principles and see how the Lord has graciously grown you in your faith and blessed you through your obedience to His Word.

One of my favorite passages in the Bible is Genesis 24:27. We see God leading Abraham's servant, Eliezer, to the woman God intended to be Isaac's wife. Because Eliezer was in the exact place God wanted him to be, he found Rebekah for Isaac. He said, "…*I being in the way, the LORD led me….*"

Looking back on my own life and ministry, I can also make the statement, "I being in the way, the Lord led me." The Bible teaches us that God will lead us step by step if we will only allow Him. Plan to live by the principles of the Bible, and He will bless you beyond your greatest imagination. He promises us in 1 Corinthians 2:9, "*But as it is written, Eye hath not seen, nor ear heard, neither have entered into the heart of man, the things which God hath prepared for them that love him.*"

PRINCIPLE ONE:

RELATIONSHIPS ARE MORE IMPORTANT THAN FAME OR THINGS.

Lay not up for yourselves treasures upon earth, where moth and rust doth corrupt, and where thieves break through and steal: But lay up for yourselves treasures in heaven, where neither moth nor rust doth corrupt, and where thieves do not break through nor steal.
—MATTHEW 6:19–20

1

RELATIONSHIPS ARE MORE IMPORTANT THAN FAME OR THINGS.

In the first part of Matthew 6, the Lord is speaking to His disciples about material possessions. In essence, He was teaching them not to be overly concerned with accumulating a lot of "things."

Material possessions have a short lifespan. A thief can steal them; a natural disaster can destroy them; a tiny insect can eat through them. More importantly, when we die, we cannot take these things with us. We have yet to see a hearse towing a U-Haul! Anything we call ours—clothes, houses, automobiles—will eventually decay or burn. Anything I can call mine will *not* be mine one day.

When a person of wealth dies, we sometimes wonder, "How much did he leave?" The answer is always the same: "He left it all!" Our possessions can be taken away from us at any time, and eventually they all *will be* in one way or another! Things on this earth will only last for a brief period of time.

We should not spend our lives trying to make a name for ourselves. Fame is short-lived. There is no guarantee that yesterday's heroes will be known by today's generation. When I speak in high school chapels or to young men across the country, I sometimes mention names like Stan Musial, Ted Williams, and Enos Slaughter. All I get from these young people are blank stares. These names mean absolutely nothing to them. These were all famous baseball players in my day. In the same way, Barry Bonds may be a household name today, but his fame will probably not carry over to the next generation.

Relationships are far more important than things or fame. It is important for us to learn to prioritize our relationships and not be overly concerned with possessions or reputation. We must look to the Bible, the Word of God, to get the proper perspective.

OUR RELATIONSHIP WITH GOD

The one relationship that should take precedence over all others is our relationship with God. This begins at the moment we receive Jesus as our Saviour. It is the single-most important decision an individual will ever make. In John 3:7, Jesus says, "...*ye must be born again.*" In Acts 16:31, Paul tells a Philippian jailer to "...*Believe on the Lord Jesus Christ, and thou shalt be saved....*" First John 5:13

says, "*These things have I written unto you that believe on the name of the Son of God; that ye may know that ye have eternal life, and that ye may believe on the name of the Son of God.*"

What a blessing it is to be one hundred percent sure that you are a child of God and on your way to Heaven! In Galatians 3:26, we are assured, "*For ye are all the children of God by faith in Christ Jesus.*"

Perhaps you had the privilege of being born into a Christian home, but birth into a Christian family is not a ticket to Heaven. Salvation is not inherited. You get to Heaven by being born again—that is, by putting your trust in the Lord and accepting Him as Saviour. God doesn't have any grandchildren, just children, and every man is responsible to make this choice before God.

Years ago, I was preaching at a Bible college in Virginia. I made a statement about the church of the Lord Jesus Christ and the early disciples. I said, "Judas walked with the Lord three years and yet was not saved. If someone could walk in close proximity with Jesus and that first group of disciples and still not be saved, it is possible for a student to enter Bible college and not be saved." After I preached the message, a young man came to me and said he wasn't sure he was saved. That afternoon, after going through the Gospel message with him, he trusted Christ as his Saviour.

Have you committed your soul to the Lord? It does you no good to commit it to the church or to a preacher.

In order to be saved, you must entrust your soul to the Lord. Only the Lord Jesus Christ can save you.

Salvation is a glorious experience; however, it is only the beginning of a wonderful relationship with God. He wants us to maintain a daily walk with Him and to fellowship with Him—learning His laws and experiencing a close relationship with Him.

Many years ago, I made a decision to make my relationship with God my first priority. I chose to live daily by this principle. Walking with Him day by day has given me courage and stability that nothing else could produce.

Psalm 46:1 says, "*God is our refuge and strength, a very present help in trouble.*" It doesn't matter what happens to us when God is our refuge. When we continually feed on the Word, meditate on its precepts, and apply them to our lives, we grow strong in our faith and in our fellowship with God.

The Bible says, "*…faith cometh by hearing, and hearing by the word of God*" (Romans 10:17). The more we read the Bible, the more God will give us grace sufficient for the day. The closer we are to the Lord, the more we realize that He is all we need for every situation that comes into our lives.

A daily walk with God will also bring us peace. Philippians 4:7 speaks of "*the peace of God, which passeth all understanding.*" What a wonderful Saviour we have! We are not only saved by His grace, but we also know the meaning of true peace as we commune with Him on a continual basis.

May I urge you to make your walk with God your first and foremost priority? The remaining principles we will study must be built upon this foundation. Nothing can replace your personal relationship with God. Give your first time, your best time, to Him. Draw close to Him and allow Him to draw close to you. *"Be still, and know that I am God…"* (Psalm 46:10).

OUR RELATIONSHIP WITH FAMILY

The second priority is our relationship to our families. We may sometimes be tempted to rearrange the sequence of our priorities and think that ministry is more important than family. It is sad when folks have to learn the hard way that losing one's family means losing one's ministry, as well. God never commands us to place our ministries before our families, and doing so is not only dangerous, it is dishonoring to God.

Within the family are three critical relationships— husband/wife, sibling/sibling, and parent/child. By far, the most important of these is the husband/wife relationship. No other human relationship should be given priority over this sacred union! No co-worker, friend, extended family, or child should take precedence over your spouse.

In Genesis 2, God brings Adam into a deep sleep and, from his rib, creates woman. Verse 24 states, "*Therefore shall a man leave his father and his mother, and shall cleave unto his wife: and they shall be one flesh.*" God's design is that once married, that new relationship takes greater importance over all other human acquaintances. Other relationships must take a back seat. This principle of "leaving and cleaving" is a principle of marriage that is meant to last forever.

Developing a meaningful marriage involves time and work, but it is well worth the effort. It is easy to neglect a spouse when time and energy are invested into raising children. As a result, many couples find that once their kids have grown and left the nest, their marriage relationship has drifted apart and has become very weak over the years.

Healthy, loving relationships are strengthened through hard work. There is no easy, fast-track formula for a strong and successful marriage. Nurturing a strong marriage relationship is something that takes years of steadfast commitment.

God intended for the marriage relationship to be the closest relationship on earth. When we put our children first, we lose our balance. That does not please the Lord, and it makes for a very frustrating life.

Our next priority is children. Psalm 127:3 says, "*Lo, children are an heritage of the LORD: and the fruit of the womb is his reward.*" Ephesians 6:1–4 gives sound advice for children and parents alike. Children are to honor their parents. Fathers are not to provoke their children to wrath, but should bring them up in the nurture and admonition of the Lord.

My wife and I had not yet started Bible college when the Lord blessed us with our first child, Renee. Eight years later, God gave us our son, Tim. Early on, we began having family devotions daily in an effort to keep our relationship with our children a priority.

It is not innate in children to be obedient to their parents! Obedience is a principle that must be taught consistently. Effective training and mentoring involves spending time with our children. As our daughter, Renee, got older, she and I had several opportunities to spend time with each other, because we drove to school together. (I was teaching at a public school at that time, and Renee was a student at the same school.)

On the mission field, we always set Saturday morning aside for family time. We'd have a Kentucky breakfast complete with biscuits and chocolate gravy (the recipe came from Virginia's mom). We would then do something together—such as play a board game, go bowling, take a walk in the park, or engage in some other interesting activity.

In addition to this, we participated in all of the church and school activities. Our children loved to go to church every time the door was open. To them, attending church and church events was never a bore or drudgery; it was a privilege and a joy. (Renee and Tim also became very close while we were in Japan as they traveled back and forth, to and from school on a train.)

Tim and I would spend time playing basketball and other sports whenever we could. My wife and Renee would cook and sew together. Sometimes, we'd invite other missionary families to our home for good fellowship, food, and games.

One of the great tragedies today is that parents simply do not know their children. They live under one roof, but are strangers to one another. As the primary breadwinners, dads spend most of their time working. They get home exhausted and hoping for peace and quiet. If dads are not careful, they could very easily just plop down on their easy chairs with the remote in hand and hardly say two sentences to their children.

Some moms must return to work soon after their children are born. Juggling motherhood, a job, and household responsibilities can rob them of time that should be spent with the children.

Spending very little time with our children is not God's will for our families. One of the reasons for the high rate of juvenile delinquency is that children need love and attention, and it is not being provided within their own families. We are also losing Christian young people from faithful families because parents are neglecting this vital relationship in a pursuit of lesser things.

If you do not have a right relationship with your family, your ministry will suffer greatly! The two go hand-in-hand. You cannot honor God in ministry while you dishonor Him in your home.

OUR RELATIONSHIP WITH THE CHURCH

I believe our third most important relationship is with God's people in the local church. Hebrews 10:25 states, *"Not forsaking the assembling of ourselves together, as the manner of some is; but exhorting one another: and so much the more, as ye see the day approaching."*

Attending church must be a regular occurrence in your life. This is what God has intended. You should not contemplate over a decision of whether or not you will be in your place. Be excited about getting to the house of God every Sunday morning, Sunday night, Wednesday night, and special events, such as revival, missions conference, and soulwinning and visitation opportunities.

Church attendance is the only way we can obey God while developing strong relationships with our pastor and church family. First Corinthians 12 teaches that the church is like a body, and we are members of that body. We must place a high importance on our relationship with the church, God's institution for worldwide evangelism.

This priority is one that God will bless in your life. Jesus died for the church! God places great value—a high priority—on His people gathering together and worshipping Him. He will honor you as you honor Him in this aspect of your life.

OUR RELATIONSHIP WITH OUR OCCUPATION

Our fourth relational priority deals with our occupation. For a Bible-believing Christian, this role should always follow family and ministry. God cares far more about you and the welfare of your relationships than He does about how you earn a paycheck!

Ephesians 6:5–7 refer to the master/servant relationship, but the principles given apply to our modern day employer/employee relationships, as well. Paul admonishes in these verses, "*Servants, be obedient to them that are your masters according to the flesh, with fear and trembling, in singleness of your heart, as unto Christ; Not with eyeservice, as menpleasers; but as the servants of Christ, doing the will of God from the heart; With good will doing service, as to the Lord, and not to men.*"

We should not shirk from our duties as employees. We are commanded in Colossians 3:23–24 to be good workers wherever God places us—doing our labor as unto the Lord, not with eye-service, as men-pleasers. We are to realize our labor is not for a paycheck or for an employer. It is first for the Lord and ought to be done for His glory, for we are His workmanship! Your labor, regardless of what it is, is a direct reflection of your Saviour!

Slavery was a large establishment in Paul's day, yet he taught the slaves to be obedient to their masters, serving them as unto the Lord. You may be working for someone else, but if you work as unto the Lord, it will make a huge difference in your work ethic! Truly, there is no greater motivation or higher call than to do something as unto the Lord!

OUR RELATIONSHIP TO THOSE WHO ARE LOST

There is one final critical relationship God gives to each Christian: our relationship with those who are lost.

In Luke 15:2, the scribes and Pharisees were trying to find cause to accuse Jesus and murmured, "...*This man receiveth sinners, and eateth with them.*" They thought they had finally caught him doing something wrong. But if Jesus did not receive sinners, where would we be? We would be condemned to spend eternity in hell.

Throughout Scripture, God encourages us to seek the lost and share the Gospel with them. We should not neglect our responsibility to tell others about Jesus Christ. Yes, we are to be separated from the world, but not isolated from the lost! We are the salt and light of the world. We must develop relationships with the unsaved, so that they can see Jesus in us.

Possessions and popularity will pass away, but Christ-honoring relationships will last for eternity. I believe our relationship with Him in Heaven will be contingent upon our relationship with Him while we're on earth. Someone once said, "What I do with His Son determines *where* I will spend eternity. What I do with what He puts in my hands will determine *how* I spend eternity." There are rewards in Heaven even as there are degrees in hell. So, how are you going to spend your eternity? How are you progressing in developing these critical relationships that God has given to you?

This first principle is vital if you intend to stand before Christ and hear, "Well done, thou good and faithful servant!" These roles and relationships are God-given priorities for your life. If you neglect them, you do so to your own peril.

By now you may be wondering, "With all I have to do, how can I properly address each of these God-given relationships?" How do we effectively balance our lives to carry out all that we're supposed to accomplish?

Years ago, I read a book entitled, *Spiritual Leadership*, by J. Oswald Sanders. Outside of the Bible, this book has been one of the most helpful books I've ever read. In it, Mr. Sanders made this profound statement, "God has given us all the time we need to do everything He wants us to do."

When I read that statement, my first thought was, "Evidently, I am doing a lot of things He doesn't want me to do." Spend your time with eternity in mind. Ask yourself if a particular pursuit or project is going to count for eternity. More importantly, ask yourself if you are giving your best time and energy to the most important relationships in your life. We can easily be consumed with things that don't matter or with promoting ourselves up the wrong ladder. In doing so, we fail to have time for the roles that really do matter and the people God has placed in our lives to love and nurture.

God has blessed you with enough time and energy to effectively accomplish everything He desires for you to do. He blesses those whose relationships are right before Him, and He promises to take care of everything else!

PRINCIPLE ONE:
*Relationships
are more important
than fame or things.*

*This is my commandment,
That ye love one another,
as I have loved you.*
—JOHN 15:12

PRINCIPLE TWO:

NOTHING ANYONE CAN DO TO ME CAN HARM ME; ONLY MY REACTION WILL HARM ME.

And we know that all things work together for good to them that love God, to them who are the called according to his purpose.
—Romans 8:28

2

NOTHING ANYONE CAN DO TO ME CAN HARM ME; ONLY MY REACTION WILL HARM ME.

God allowed a very difficult situation to come into my life to teach me this principle. Several years ago, I was in the midst of a "battle" with other preachers and missionaries. (Missionaries have interpersonal problems, just like everyone else!) Those problems caused me to do a lot of questioning and made me feel that I had been wronged by some people. Looking back, I believe the devil was trying to destroy my spirit toward life and ministry through these circumstances.

It's amazing how the providence of God is manifested just when you need it! Somebody had given me a booklet called *Your Reactions Are Showing*. That little book spoke to my heart, because of how it related to what I was dealing with in that moment. It emphasized that people and circumstances will not harm us. These things *hurt*, but they cannot *harm*. Only our reactions have the potential to harm us.

In response to this truth, I began reading and studying my Bible, which allowed me to see the situation from God's perspective. I came to grips with the fact that injustice was not the source of my heart's problems, but it was my improper reaction that created a defeated spirit within me. I realized that while I did not have the power to stop people and situations from hurting me, I did have the power to control my reactions to them.

I praise the Lord that all who were involved in that misunderstanding are very close friends to this day! Had I remained angry and bitter, I would have hindered God's working in my life, and I would not have experienced the blessing of those friendships.

Romans 8:28 promises, "...*all things work together for good to them that love God, to them who are the called according to his purpose.*" Every situation that God allows to come into our lives is for our good and for His purpose.

Just the other day, a young lad said to me, "I don't know why I have to take all these math and English classes. All I want to do is preach!" God is sovereign, even during times of difficulty and stretching. He is constantly at work in every circumstance of our lives. He is always growing us and teaching us. I'm sure that somewhere down the line, that young fellow who "just wanted to preach" will be able to use the college courses he was once reluctant to take, and he will be grateful that he learned from them.

Suffering is a fact of life. The righteous suffer as do the wicked. Job says in chapter 14, verse 1, "*Man that is born of a woman is of few days, and full of trouble.*" In 2 Corinthians 1:8, the Apostle Paul talks of despairing life itself: "*For we would not, brethren, have you ignorant of our trouble which came to us in Asia, that we were pressed out of measure, above strength, insomuch that we despaired even of life.*" Moses, Elijah, and Jonah were men also greatly used of God, but each reached a point of despondency that drove them to ask God to take their lives.

Trials come to *every* person. "Prosperity evangelism" may appear to be a convincing philosophy, but it is not a biblical concept. This teaching claims that if you are right with God, you will always be wealthy, healthy, and well-liked. While this idea may sound good, it is simply not the truth.

Pain, struggles, and conflicts can be difficult to understand while you're going through them. It can also be easy to compare your problems with the prosperity of others. Psalm 73:3 and 17 provide this encouragement, "*For I was envious at the foolish, when I saw the prosperity of the wicked. Until I went into the sanctuary of God; then understood I their end.*"

The suffering of the righteous is only for a season. It will pass. God has not promised a pain-free or trial-free life, but He does provide grace for every believer. He does promise a "light at the end of the tunnel"! In 2 Corinthians 12, we read of Paul asking God to remove the thorn in his flesh. God did not answer Paul's prayer the way he anticipated, but in verse 9, He says to Paul, "…*My grace is sufficient for thee: for my strength is made perfect in weakness.*"

First Peter 2:9 refers to believers as a "peculiar" people, "*But ye are a chosen generation, a royal priesthood, an holy nation, a peculiar people; that ye should shew forth the praises of him who hath called you out of darkness into his marvellous light.*" The word *peculiar* means "chosen" or "encircled." Draw a dot with a circle around it. The dot symbolizes the Christian, and the circle represents God. We are God's encircled people. All circumstances that take place in our lives are God-filtered. The devil could not touch Job until he got permission from God to do so. In the same way, nothing can get to us unless it comes from God or through God.

Circumstances will hurt us. Unsaved people will hurt us, and fellow believers will hurt us. There will be squabbles and misunderstandings, and there will be situations in which we are unjustly accused. We cannot stop these things from taking place, but we can determine our responses.

How we respond to adversities determines our usefulness to Christ. The Bible gives us the responses of two men in adversity: Joseph and Ahithophel. One reacted properly. The other reacted improperly.

The story of Joseph is an excellent illustration of how adversity should be handled. When studying the life of Joseph, you will not find him reacting in a negative manner, yet people were mistreating him and wrongly accusing him on every side.

When his brothers tried to kill him and failed, they sold him into slavery. When he became a servant to Potiphar, he could have had a horrible attitude and sulked at his misfortunes, but he chose to maintain his good testimony. Consequently, he was given oversight of Potiphar's household. Potiphar entrusted all that he had to Joseph.

Then, Potiphar's wife tried to seduce Joseph, but he fled in the face of evil. Joseph left his coat behind in the hands of Potiphar's wife, but he didn't lose his integrity. Joseph was falsely accused of rape and was thrown into prison.

Do you think Joseph held a pity party while in jail? It doesn't appear that way! He kept a good attitude and did not seek revenge or become bitter. Others had hurt him, but it did not harm him. He chose to respond to his circumstances with grace.

Have you ever heard the saying, "The cream always rises to the top"? If you have milked a cow before, you must have noticed that the cream, which is the best part of the milk, always rises to the top, while the lesser particles sink to the bottom. This is where we get the phrase *cream of the crop*, which means, "the best of the best." Joseph "rose to the top" in every situation.

After Joseph was thrown into the pit, falsely accused, and wrongfully imprisoned, the time came for Joseph to reside in the palace of Pharaoh. Pharaoh had a dream that no one could interpret. His chief butler remembered Joseph and his ability to interpret dreams, so Joseph was summoned from prison. Pharaoh was so impressed by Joseph's good attitude and abilities that he made him prime minister of Egypt.

Joseph's biggest test came when he was second in command over the entire kingdom. When he could have taken revenge on his brothers, he refused to do so. He did not take the place of God, as he says in Genesis 50:19–20, *"…Fear not for am I in the place of God? But as for you, ye thought evil against me; but God meant it unto good, to bring to pass, as it is this day, to save much people alive."*

Joseph consistently did what was right, and God rewarded him. He could not control his circumstances but controlled his response. Because Joseph's reactions were pleasing to the Lord, God blessed and used him in a mighty way.

Ahithophel is an example of a person who reacted improperly. When Ahithophel, David's chief counselor (1 Chronicles 27:33), gave David advice, it was as if God Himself was giving counsel (2 Samuel 16:23). He and David had a wonderful, close relationship; however, when David's son, Absalom, rebelled against David, Ahithophel changed sides and became Absalom's counselor. He said to Absalom, "If you give me enough men, I will kill David." What would cause someone to switch loyalties that quickly? What made Ahithophel change?

Ahithophel was the father of Eliam, who was the father of Bathsheba (2 Samuel 11:3 and 23:34). Did Ahithophel have every right to be angry? Yes, he did. David sinned when he lusted after Bathsheba, Uriah's wife. As a result of his adultery, he had Bathsheba's husband killed in battle. I believe that Ahithophel allowed his anger to fester within him all those years. I believe he was enraged at David for destroying his family and could not find it in his heart to forgive. Hatred and unforgiveness gave way to bitterness. Ahithophel's reaction of bitterness ruined his life, and in the end, he committed suicide.

Both Joseph and Ahithophel faced adversities. One's reaction led him to commit suicide. The other's response promoted him to become a prime minister.

Friend, your reactions are showing! You may feel that you have just cause to be angry with a person or a situation, but you do not have the right to become bitter. You cannot afford to give place to bitterness in your heart. When bitterness creeps into your life, it will keep you from effectively serving the Lord. Remember that the devil does not care what he uses; he just wants you to be bitter.

Vengeance is not our business; it is God's business. When we try to avenge a hurt, we are actually removing God from His rightful place and putting ourselves there. Romans 12:19 admonishes, *"Dearly beloved, avenge not yourselves, but rather give place unto wrath: for it is written, Vengeance is mine; I will repay, saith the Lord."*

We will get hurt when the trials come, but if we handle them properly, God can use us in a mighty way. Although I was in the midst of a difficult situation with other missionaries, God turned it around to teach me a valuable lesson. I had to rely on His wisdom and grace to be able to respond correctly.

Going through that particular difficulty while serving in Japan taught me how to minister to others who were going through the same battles. Despite the tough times, God was sovereign in bringing about His plan for the people of Kobe and Osaka, Japan. By His grace and through His strength, we were able to establish two independent Baptist churches and a Bible school to train Japanese men for the ministry.

God used that trial to humble me and to teach me to depend on Him for everything. I was able to emerge from a bad situation by ridding myself of pride and asking the Lord to fill me with His Spirit.

What has God allowed into your life? Slander? Attack? Gossip? Perhaps He has allowed hurt or heartbreak. Nothing you can do will remove the pain, but you can determine what it will produce within you. You must make a choice. Choose a right response before God. Choose to honor Him, and He will honor you!

PRINCIPLE TWO:
*Nothing anyone can do to me
can harm me; only my reaction
will harm me.*

*And we know that all things work together for
good to them that love God, to them who are
the called according to his purpose.*
—ROMANS 8:28

PRINCIPLE THREE:

IT IS MORE BLESSED TO GIVE
THAN TO RECEIVE.

*I have shewed you all things, how that so labouring
ye ought to support the weak, and to remember
the words of the Lord Jesus, how he said, It is more
blessed to give than to receive.*
—ACTS 20:35

3

IT IS MORE BLESSED TO GIVE
THAN TO RECEIVE.

It was at a missions conference in Detroit, Michigan, when God indelibly impressed this third principle on my heart. The pastor who preached was a godly man by the name of Dr. Overby. He was greatly used of God in many ways, particularly in the area of missions.

At that time, I was tithing and practicing faith-promise giving, but as I sat in the audience and listened to Dr. Overby preach on Luke 6:38, God developed within my heart a new level of appreciation and understanding of this principle. The verse says, "*Give, and it shall be given unto you; good measure, pressed down, and shaken together, and running over, shall men give into your bosom. For with the same measure that ye mete withal it shall be measured to you again.*"

During his message, Dr. Overby shared of a time in his life when he had meager means and owned only one suit. A lady came to him one day and said, "Brother Overby, my husband just passed away, and the Lord has laid on my heart to give you his suits. He has several good suits. If you could wear them, I'd like to give them to you."

Dr. Overby asked the lady if she was sure God wanted her to give the suits to him, and when she assured him, Dr. Overby responded, "Well, if He did, then they will fit me because the Lord knows my size." He was right! The jackets fit perfectly, and so did the trousers! I sensed a sincere joy in this man. He knew how to give of himself and of his resources to others, and he knew how to trust God to provide for his needs.

In Acts 20:35, Jesus says, *"It is more blessed to give than to receive."* When I read this verse, I realized that Jesus gave more than anybody else gave. He owns everything. The Bible says in Colossians 1:16, *"…All things were created by Him and for Him."* He left the glory of Heaven and came to earth to take upon Himself the sins of the world. Other men die because of their sins, but Jesus, the perfect, sinless Lamb, died for all of our sins. No one knew more about giving than Jesus did.

Today's predominant philosophy on giving is the opposite of what Jesus teaches. To many, it is better to *get* than to *give*. If you want to prove this statement, try standing in front of Wal-Mart with ten five-dollar bills. Say to people as they come in, "I have in my hand a five-dollar bill. If you would like, I'll give you this bill, but if you prefer, you could give me five dollars." I guarantee, you'll end up giving away every five-dollar bill, and no one will give you a five-dollar bill!

Referring back to Acts 20:35, the Apostle Paul is speaking to the elders at the church in Ephesus. The last admonition he gave was, "…*Remember the words of the Lord Jesus, how he said, It is more blessed to give than to receive.*"

When we hear someone make an unusual, hard-to-believe claim we often ask ourselves, "Does he really know what he is talking about? Has it worked for him?"

When we were on furlough from Japan, we lived in an apartment in Rossville, Georgia. A student who was going to Japan as a missionary was interested in viewing our slides, so Virginia and I invited him and his wife over to our apartment. My wife baked a double-chocolate cake (my favorite) and prepared a pot of coffee. We had forgotten that these people claimed to be health buffs!

Fortunately, our guests didn't want to offend us, so the husband ate a large piece of chocolate cake and drank a cup of coffee. Before the evening was over, he tried to convince us of the value of health food. I listened for a while but thought, "If health food truly did its job, why are some of his family members always sick?" I said to him, "Since it doesn't seem to help your family a whole lot, you would have to engage in a battle to persuade me of the merits." When someone makes a bold statement like that student did, he ought to be able to back it up with results!

I remember going to a mall with two other preachers some time ago. We came across a fellow manning a little stand full of products designed to improve the texture and health of the skin. I looked at the vendor's face and noticed that it was red and blotchy. It was just a mess! I asked him if he himself had used the products. He affirmed that he had. All I could think was, "Man, if he uses this stuff, then I don't want it!"

Well, I have good news for you. Jesus can back up His strong statements about giving! What does Jesus know about giving? Second Corinthians 8:9 states, "*For ye know the grace of our Lord Jesus Christ, that, though he was rich, yet for your sakes he became poor, that ye through his poverty might be rich.*" Jesus exemplified that the person who lives to *give* is happier than the person who lives to *get*.

Another great example of giving is found in 1 Chronicles 29. David is gathering materials for the great temple of God. He wanted to build the temple himself, but God had someone else in mind for this task. Although David's son Solomon would build it, God allowed David the privilege of collecting all the needed materials. In verse 7, we find these words: "*And gave for the service of the house of God of gold five thousand talents and ten thousand drams, and of silver ten thousand talents, and of brass eighteen thousand talents, and one hundred thousand talents of iron.*" If you calculate the gold and silver that was given for the construction of the temple, it would be equivalent to about $2.5 billion in today's currency! The children of Israel gave generously.

How else should we give? First Chronicles 29 further illustrates the spirit and attitude we should have toward giving: *"And they with whom precious stones were found gave them...."* They gave sacrificially.

Then, the Bible says in verse 9, *"Then the people rejoiced, for that they offered willingly, because with perfect heart they offered willingly to the LORD: and David the king also rejoiced with great joy."* They gave willingly and joyfully.

True giving is generous, sacrificial, willing, and joyful. I learned to give as a young Christian, but my giving has taken on a new level of faith and obedience since I heard the preaching of that dear pastor in 1968. I can honestly say that God's blessings in our lives have been exceeding and abundant! When a person gives in the way God commands, the results will truly boggle the mind!

One of the best decisions Virginia and I have made was to join Lancaster Baptist Church. This is a place where God is blessing tremendously because of the willingness of the members to give sacrificially. Not long after we became members, the church held its annual stewardship banquet. At that time, I was out of town due to prior preaching commitments, but Virginia stayed home in Lancaster. She listened to the weekly messages on giving. When it was time for us to discuss the amount we would give, I was so touched that my wife came up with an amount much bigger than mine. She had heard the Word of God and was responding with a willing, joyful heart!

When we properly give, it provokes God's pleasure. Isn't it wonderful to know we can do things that please God? God loves a cheerful giver.

Proper giving perpetuates God's provisions. In Luke 6:38, God promises abundant blessings to those who give. Galatians 6:7 says, "*Be not deceived; God is not mocked: for whatsoever a man soweth, that shall he also reap.*"

When *you* put in a teaspoonful, *God* gives back a tablespoonful. If you give a tablespoonful, God will give back a shovel full. If you put in a shovel full, He'll put in a truckload! Is there a limit to giving? Sure. When God's resources run out, it's over, but we haven't even begun to scratch the surface of God's resources!

Giving with the right attitude protects God's people. The Bible states that where your treasure is, there will your heart be also! Giving to the Lord provides protection from jealousy, greed, and pride. While this principle applies to financial giving, it also applies to giving of time and talent to the Lord's work. The person who lives to give is much happier than the person who lives to get. Sincere, joyful giving protects the heart, and helps maintain a close relationship with God.

This is a great principle! Once you put God to the test, you will never lack for anything you need, and you will find that God is much better at taking care of you than you could take care of yourself! Give faithfully. Give joyfully. Give cheerfully. Give willingly. Establish your life upon this principle, and watch God fulfill His promises in your life!

PRINCIPLE THREE:
*It is more blessed to give
than to receive.*

*Give, and it shall be given unto you; good
measure, pressed down, and shaken together,
and running over, shall men give into your
bosom. For with the same measure that ye
mete withal it shall be measured to you again.*
—LUKE 6:38

PRINCIPLE FOUR:

EACH PERSON IS A CREATION
OF GOD AND IS UNIQUE.

*Before I formed thee in the belly I knew
thee; and before thou camest forth out of
the womb I sanctified thee, and I ordained
thee a prophet unto the nations.*
—JEREMIAH 1:5

4

EACH PERSON IS A CREATION
OF GOD AND IS UNIQUE.

In Jeremiah 1:5, we see God preparing Jeremiah for a special ministry. He was to be God's primary prophet to the nation of Israel. Isn't our God awesome? Long before we were born, He knew us. God had His eye on us while we were yet being formed in our mothers' wombs!

No one is an "accident." God created us and fashioned us after His own image. He has a purpose for each of us. From conception, a fetus is a living soul.

A big, burly policeman came to me weeping after I had preached a sermon from this passage in Jeremiah. He told me how much it meant to him to realize that he was not an accident. Growing up, that was all he heard from his parents. It is such a tragedy when people are forced to carry the burden of feeling unloved and unwanted by their own parents!

One of our six grandchildren is adopted. My son and daughter-in-law were living in Bolivia and had been praying about adopting a child (although they already had three children at that time). Donna, my daughter-in-law, was helping out at an orphanage, when one day, a beautiful little girl walked in. She had many problems, and in her parents' eyes, she was an accident. They had abandoned her. But, in God's eyes, she was precious! God, in His infinite wisdom, would one day carry out His special plan for her life, because she was His creation. God made each of us unique for a reason.

David, in Psalm 139:14–16 exclaims, "*I will praise thee; for I am fearfully and wonderfully made: marvellous are thy works; and that my soul knoweth right well. My substance was not hid from thee, when I was made in secret, and curiously wrought in the lowest parts of the earth. Thine eyes did see my substance, yet being unperfect; and in thy book all my members were written, which in continuance were fashioned, when as yet there was none of them.*" In 1 Corinthians 12:18, the Apostle Paul writes, "*But now hath God set the members every one of them in the body, as it hath pleased him.*"

It would help us to keep this verse in mind the next time we look in the mirror and don't like the reflection looking back at us!

God not only created us, He *knows* us perfectly. First Corinthians 4:7 says, "*For who maketh thee to differ from another? and what hast thou that thou didst not receive? now if thou didst receive it, why dost thou glory, as if thou hadst not received it?"* Taking this verse seriously would do great things for a person's attitude.

First, it would eliminate all boasting. All that we are and all that we own are gifts from God. Paul said in 1 Corinthians 15:10, *"...By the grace of God, I am what I am."*

Fully grasping this verse would also eliminate all grumbling. Oh, what a world this would be if no one ever complained or grumbled! If we are not careful, we can spend our time griping about what we don't have or what we are not. As Christians, we must identify and acknowledge what God has put in our hands and thank Him for creating us.

I was born in rural Kentucky. We ate potatoes in some form or another with all our meals. My mom had 101 recipes for potatoes! As a boy, I wondered why we were so poor, but God had a purpose that I could not see. In Japan, rice is the staple food. I had never eaten rice in my life before moving to Japan. When I arrived there as a missionary, I had a decision to make. Either I could complain about having to eat rice, or I could learn to appreciate it. You guessed it! I learned to like rice. God used my rural upbringing to prepare me for life as a missionary.

If we take 1 Corinthians 4:7 to heart, it would also clear our hearts of jealousy. Why be jealous over someone's looks or someone's possessions? I have what God wants me to have. In all my years of living for God, I haven't run out of anything. God has always given me exactly what I need when I need it. He has continually enabled and equipped me to carry out His will for my life for His glory.

Choosing to live by the principle found in 1 Corinthians 4 would also exclude all unthankfulness. We live in a world where people take everything for granted. Fewer and fewer people stop to say "thank you."

Make it a habit to thank people who encourage you or help you along the way. Write them notes of appreciation. It would be easier to be thankful, and we would express our gratitude more often, if we lived recognizing that everything we own is from the Lord.

Be very careful not to question God for creating you a certain way: "God, why didn't You make me a blonde?" "Lord, I wish I had a petite frame." "Why am I so dumb in school?" "Why can't I sing well," or "Why wasn't I born with athletic abilities?" That's like telling God that He should have made a better version of you, and that you know better than He does! God knows everything about you. He knows your name. He knows where you are mentally, physically, emotionally, and spiritually; and He has planned it all according to His purpose for your life.

There are more than six billion people on this planet, but God knows you intimately. He will never forget about you. He knows you far better than you know yourself. He even knows the number of hairs on your head! He is omniscient, and there is no insignificant person in His eyes.

Often, when God instructs us to do something for Him, we begin to tell God about ourselves: "I'm not very smart." "I'm not very strong." Telling God about ourselves is a waste of time! He knows us. He made us.

God loves you and has sanctified you. Sanctified means that He has set you apart for a specific purpose. A good example of this word is found in the Old Testament. The articles in the tabernacle were sanctified. They were set apart for God's specific use.

In the epistles, the word most often used when referring to believers is *saint*. (The root word for sanctified is *saint*.) God's children are to be "set apart" or different from the world.

It's a mystery to me why we want to look and act like the world. First Corinthians 6:19–20 is a sobering reminder of why we should be distinctly different from the world: "*What? know ye not that your body is the temple of the Holy Ghost which is in you, which ye have of God, and ye are not your own? For ye are bought with a price: therefore glorify God in your body, and in your spirit, which are God's.*" As children of God, our purpose is to glorify Him.

I remember being on a snowmobile surrounded by four feet of snow in northern Canada. That four feet of snow consisted of perhaps billions of flakes, yet every single flake on the ground had its own unique design.

It's no news to us that our children, born into the same family, sharing the same set of parents, can be as different as night and day. My children are so different from each other and from their parents that I sometimes wonder if they're really related to us! We have traveled the world over many times, but I have yet to see two people who are exactly the same.

There is no such thing as "identical twins." There are twins who look very much alike, talk and act the same way, and even have similar mannerisms, but for certain, they have differences that set them apart. People very close to twins are able to tell them apart, because each one has a certain characteristic that the other does not possess.

Every person is unique. Out of 6.5 billion people on the face of the earth, no two individuals are exactly alike. God didn't make us from a rubber stamp! There is no mold. He doesn't need one, because He never makes mistakes!

Now, here is the key: We were uniquely formed not to *clash*, but to *complement* each other!

God has ordained each of us. In Ephesians 2:10, Paul exhorts, "*For we are his workmanship, created in Christ Jesus unto good works, which God hath before ordained that we should walk in them.*" God has ordained us to walk in good works. He also works on us, in us, and through us to change us into His image. Christians are not *sinless*, but we should *sin less* as we grow in God's grace.

God also has a specific purpose for each of us. It is not His will "*that any should perish, but that all should come to repentance*" (2 Peter 3:9). God's first purpose for us is salvation. Hell was not prepared for mankind, but for the devil and his angels. When people go to hell, they have missed God's purpose.

After salvation, God purposes for us to become fruit-bearing believers. Don't fail to participate in this God-given purpose for your life! John 15:16 states, "*Ye have not chosen me, but I have chosen you, and ordained you, that ye should go and bring forth fruit, and that your fruit should remain: that whatsoever ye shall ask of the Father in my name, he may give it you.*" Is your life manifesting the fruit of the Spirit? Are your mannerisms characterized by a spirit of love, joy, and peace?

Try this for one week: treat every person you meet as if he or she were the most important person in the world. Think of how that could change your life and the lives of others around you. God is not a respecter of persons. He didn't choose you on the basis of looks, education, success, or social status. Each person is important and significant in the eyes of God, from the homeless little boy living on the streets of Brazil to the President of the United States. Are you communicating His love and acceptance to others?

Imagine what a dull world it would be if we all looked and acted alike! God did not create robots that can't think or respond. He created unique individuals with distinctly different qualities, a free will, and an eternal purpose.

Start with yourself. Accept who you are in God's master plan. Be satisfied with how He created you, and be who He made you to be. Set aside the discontentment that arises from comparing yourself with others. Stop trying to be someone you are not, and simply accept God's plan for *you*.

Then, apply this principle to everyone you meet. Remember that each person is special to God. Each person needs the Gospel, and each person has a purpose in God's eternal plan.

PRINCIPLE FOUR:
*Each person is a creation of God
and is unique.*

*Before I formed thee in the belly I knew thee;
and before thou camest forth out of the womb
I sanctified thee, and I ordained thee a prophet
unto the nations.*
—JEREMIAH 1:5

PRINCIPLE FIVE:

HAPPINESS IS A BY-PRODUCT OF FAITHFULNESS TO GOD AND NOT A GOAL.

But godliness with contentment is great gain.
—1 Timothy 6:6

5

HAPPINESS IS A BY-PRODUCT
OF FAITHFULNESS TO GOD
AND NOT A GOAL.

The world places so much emphasis on the pursuit of happiness. People want to live *happy* lives, enjoy *happy* marriages, and maintain *happy* homes. What they often fail to realize is that happiness depends on *circumstances* and *events* surrounding their lives. If something goes wrong on Monday or something troubling pops up on Tuesday, then happiness is out of the picture. If their car doesn't start, their roof is leaking, and their son doesn't make the football team, then happiness is gone. Happiness is both temporary and fleeting, which makes it a terrible life goal.

Instead of establishing happiness as our goal, we should aim for *joy*. True joy is a product of a right heart relationship with Jesus Christ. Joy does not depend on external circumstances; it is the result of the Holy Spirit dwelling in us.

I love the book of Philippians. It speaks of joy from the first chapter to the last chapter. Philippians 4:4 admonishes us to *"rejoice in the Lord alway."* It's true that we can't always rejoice in circumstances, but we *can* always rejoice in the Lord.

In Philippians 4, Paul urges us not to be anxious or worried and gives instructions for maintaining peace and joy in the Christian life.

True inner joy is a state of mind and cannot be found in a geographical location, in a possession, or in a person. Some people may think that if they could live in a place with better climate, atmosphere, and scenery, they would be happy. Some think they would be happy if they owned the latest technological gadgets, and others think if a certain person would only reciprocate their feelings, then they'd truly be happy. These thoughts are deceptive, and they distract us from the true source of joy—the Lord Jesus Christ.

We recently relocated to Lancaster, California, to base our missions efforts and to participate in training young people for the mission field. Before moving to the west, we had a nice, comfortable home in Tennessee. We loved the climate; we had our friends living nearby, and we enjoyed our surroundings.

Yet, in 2003, Virginia and I sensed that God was leading us to move to Lancaster. Our friends and acquaintances could not understand why we would want to move to the desert in our retirement years; however, we did not come out west to pursue an easier life. In fact, I would refer to the busyness of the staff and the church by teasing Pastor Chappell, "I would join this church, but I don't think I'm physically up to it!"

Quite honestly, we gave up the comforts of home and everything that was familiar to us in order to follow God's leading. We have learned over the years that joy is found in the will of God, and we've learned to pursue *Him* rather than happiness. This realization made our transition one of peace and excitement.

You see, joy does not depend on circumstances or environment. Joy is dependent on being where God wants you to be and doing what God wants you to do!

There are hundreds of books written on the topic of happiness and how to attain it, but people everywhere still look miserable! They search for happiness in all the wrong places, and often come to the conclusion that if they had more "things" they would be happier, yet the Lord Jesus Christ plainly teaches that life does not consist in the abundance of things we possess. In Luke 12:15, God warns us about the dangers of covetousness: "...*Take heed, and beware of covetousness: for a man's life consisteth not in the abundance of the things which he possesseth.*" Material possessions do not ensure happiness!

In 2 Timothy 1:7, the Apostle Paul addresses Timothy regarding timidity, another barrier to true joy: "*For God hath not given us the spirit of fear; but of power, and of love, and of a sound mind.*" We live in a world filled with fear. The unemployed fear not getting a job; the employed fear losing the job. Married couples fear divorce; singles fear never marrying. The healthy fear sickness; the sick fear not getting well. It is a universal characteristic of people to fear the unknown.

Yet, *"God hath not given us the spirit of fear…."* It is not His will for us to be confused, frustrated, or worried. He has promised to give us power, love, and a sound mind. A sound mind can be interpreted as common sense or good thinking. As we grow in the Word of God, we come to understand that the stability and peace we deeply crave is only found in Jesus Christ.

Verse 6 of Philippians 4 advises us, *"Be careful for nothing; but in every thing by prayer and supplication with thanksgiving let your requests be made known unto God."* God says, "Don't be worried or anxious about *anything*!" Circumstances and people may fail us, but if our focus is on the Lord, we'll have that inner joy He promises. The secret to finding this true happiness lies in being in the center of God's will. Day by day, we must trust Him and aim to please Him in all we do.

The opposite of joy and peace is worry and doubt. It is obvious from the verses contained in Scripture that God intends for us to be free from fear. He desires for us to experience His abiding joy and abundant life.

In Philippians 4, the Apostle Paul gives us three ways to avoid worry. **First, we can overcome worry by proper praying.** Someone has said, "More things have been accomplished by prayer than anyone will ever know." We can do a lot more *after* we pray, but we can't do more *until* we pray. We can conquer our worries and fears through prayer by casting our cares upon Him.

The Bible exhorts us to pray at all times—to pray "without ceasing." Praying without ceasing does not refer to staying in your prayer closet all day long on your knees before God. It simply means we are to have constant communion with Him. We are to be conscious of His presence in our lives and come to the place where we continually rely on Him moment by moment. If we are aware of Jesus' presence, we will continually be thinking of Him and talking to Him. As we go about our day—whether driving to work, running an errand, or sitting in office meetings—we will practice God's presence.

There may be trivial matters in our lives that we think the Lord doesn't want to be bothered with, but if it's important to us, it's important to our Heavenly Father! We must pray about everything—from big problems to small concerns! As we develop a pattern of casting our cares on the Lord, we will find that He truly is all we need. As we consume ourselves with Him, we will discover that there's no place left in our hearts for worry, and we'll experience a joy beyond compare!

The second way to overcome worry and attain true joy is through right thinking. Our problems are often caused by warped perceptions and thought processes. Most of us need a "check-up from the neck up"! We can overcome anxiety and frustration if our hearts and minds are right with God and in line with His truth.

It's impossible to think wrong and do right. We all have the power to choose how we think and what we meditate on. Determine to follow Paul's admonition in Philippians 4:8: "*Finally, brethren, whatsoever things are true, whatsoever things are honest, whatsoever things are just, whatsoever things are pure, whatsoever things are lovely, whatsoever things are of good report; if there be any virtue, and if there be any praise, think on these things.*" In order to experience the peace of God, we must fill our minds with the right thoughts and involve ourselves in the right activities. Occupy your mind with the list found in verse 8. Jesus is all of these adjectives and more!

Finally, worry can be conquered by living the way we ought to live. Verse 9 of Philippians 4 continues, "*Those things, which ye have both learned, and received, and heard, and seen in me, do: and the God of peace shall be with you.*" It is not sufficient to pray right and think right; we must also *do* right. When all is said and done, there is more *said* than *done*. Quite often we do not live up to the privileges and opportunities that God puts in our paths. We neglect to do what we know is right, and as a result, we disobey God and lose His peace and joy.

Are you searching for happiness? You're on the wrong path! Happiness is a terrible goal. Just about the time you think you've found it, it's gone. Rather than searching for happiness, search for *God*. Seek to be right with Him. Seek to do what He desires. Seek to fulfill His will first in your life. As you maintain a right heart before Him, joy will fill your life. You will truly be blessed, and your heart will hold a sacred delight that only God can produce.

PRINCIPLE FIVE:

Happiness is a by-product of faithfulness to God and not a goal.

But godliness with contentment is great gain.
—1 TIMOTHY 6:6

PRINCIPLE SIX:

IF I AM CAREFUL TO DO THE LITTLE THINGS WELL, THE BIG THINGS WILL TAKE CARE OF THEMSELVES.

Whatsoever thy hand findeth to do, do it with thy might; for there is no work, nor device, nor knowledge, nor wisdom, in the grave, whither thou goest.
—Ecclesiastes 9:10

6

IF I AM CAREFUL TO DO THE LITTLE THINGS WELL, THE BIG THINGS WILL TAKE CARE OF THEMSELVES.

Years ago, I was the guest speaker of a Sunday school class in Springfield, Tennessee. When the Sunday school teacher, whom I had known for some time, introduced me, he said, "I've always respected Brother Sisk because…." Uh-oh, I got a little nervous about how he was going to finish that statement. Then he continued, "…because he always keeps his shoes shined." I looked down at my shoes, and indeed, they were very shiny!

That man did not respect me because he thought I was a great preacher or teacher. He respected me because I took care of my shoes—a seemingly insignificant detail. Sometimes, the little details that we think are so unimportant are the very things that God uses in other peoples' lives.

We often dream of doing something big for God; and yes, God does use some people to accomplish great things, but even these people started by learning to do the small things well.

The Bible provides us with numerous illustrations of people who did little things with excellence. The first one that comes to mind is David. His life as a shepherd wasn't particularly exciting. It wasn't a highly coveted job for which many people competed. David probably became bored with his responsibilities, since sheep do not make great conversationalists.

The shepherd's job was sometimes difficult; he had to find water and grass for the sheep. The shepherd's job was sometimes dangerous; he had to protect and defend the sheep from wolves and other wild animals.

Yet, it was while David was tending his flock that he walked with God and wrote many of his psalms. He realized that the Lord was *his* Shepherd and worked at being the best shepherd a person could be. As a young boy, he learned to do his very best in the things that only God knew about. If he had not done this job well, do you think the Lord would have chosen him to be king of Israel?

Another example is Joseph, who had many duties that he didn't particularly desire. He was a slave in Potiphar's house, a keeper of a prison, and a dream interpreter in Pharaoh's kingdom, but he did his best in each of these small assignments. He was eventually promoted to the position of prime minister of Egypt. God was with Joseph and noticed that he gave his best efforts in even the little details.

Ecclesiastes 9:10 says, "*Whatsoever thy hand findeth to do, do it with thy might; for there is no work, nor device, nor knowledge, nor wisdom, in the grave, whither thou goest.*" This verse reminds us that we will die one day and will no longer be able to work. Until that time, we ought to be living out God's will for the *present*. No one is assured of tomorrow. God wants us to make the most of this moment by giving our best efforts to the seemingly unimportant areas in our lives.

Colossians 3:23 admonishes, "*And whatsoever ye do, do it heartily, as to the Lord, and not unto men.*" The word *heartily* means "to do something wholeheartedly or to the best of one's ability." It doesn't matter if you are a member of the church clean-up crew, a secretary or receptionist in an office, or the preacher at the pulpit. You are to do everything as unto the Lord.

The truth is this: People who master the small things will have opportunities to do bigger things. The little that we have in our hands can be transformed into a huge blessing when we ask the Lord to use it.

Remember the little boy who only had five loaves of bread and two fish? He gave up his lunch and turned it over to the Lord. When Jesus blessed it, it was enough to feed thousands of people. They even had baskets of leftovers!

The story of the widow in Mark 12:41–44 tells us that she gave everything she had to the Lord. She was poor and had only two mites, but her story, two thousand years later, continues to encourage and inspire us to give offerings to the Lord.

The widow of Zarephath was blessed beyond measure after she gave her last meal to the prophet Elijah. Naaman was healed of his leprosy because of a little servant girl who told his wife of the prophet Elisha. God uses everything and everyone, no matter how small, when it's offered to Him in a spirit of love and worship. He specializes in taking little things and giving them a miraculous impact!

The Apostle Paul was rarely appreciated, grossly underpaid, and often fulfilled a position far beneath his abilities, but he was content. He spent a great deal of his life doing things that were beneath his educational attainment and abilities, yet he was faithful in the little things. Paul realized that God gave him the ministry of spreading the Gospel to the Gentiles in spite of who he was. Before he met the Lord on the road to Damascus, Paul's main goal in life was to persecute Christians. Despite his past, the Lord used Paul to draw people unto Himself. Why? Because Paul was committed to accomplishing the little things first for the glory of God.

You will never know this side of Heaven how God will use someone you have led to the Lord or how He will bless some small deed of service that you performed unnoticed or in secret.

A preacher in Whitesville, West Virginia, worked for eighteen months and only had one convert. The preacher eventually gave up and moved on. That one convert went to Bible college, where he answered God's call to preach. Later, he went to Japan as a missionary and remained faithful to the Lord for many years. That missionary's name was Ron White. As far as anyone knows, Ron was this preacher's only convert. That West Virginia pastor probably thought he had failed, and he couldn't see the wonderful future that God had in store for his single convert. Yet, the Lord still used him in a mighty way.

Dr. W.A. Criswell's biography tells of the day when one of his assistants asked him to visit an elderly preacher in the hospital. This ailing preacher was at death's door. He wasn't successful by the world's standards, and he felt like a failure. When Dr. Criswell found out the preacher's name, he realized that this was the man who had led him to the Lord many years prior. (At that time, Dr. Criswell was pastor of the largest Baptist church in the world.) He rushed to the hospital, but he was too late. The elderly man passed away without knowing of his own influence and impact on the life of Dr. Criswell. Praise the Lord, in Heaven he now knows that God used him to do a great thing for the cause of Christ.

During our first service in Japan, in February of 1966, eleven people raised their hands at the end of the service indicating that they wanted to trust Christ as their Saviour. One of those men was Sogoro Ogawa. He was the first to be baptized, to have a Christian wedding, to answer the call of Christ, and to graduate from Bible school. He now serves as pastor of the largest Baptist church in Japan.

Praise God for the work He is still doing through the lives of the Ogawa family! If Sogoro Ogawa had been the only reason God sent us to Japan, he would have been worth all the sacrifice and investment!

Through my many years of traveling, I have been a guest in preachers' homes. If the pastor had kids, I would often play board games with them or shoot hoops with the boys. There is nothing like seeing children's faces light up when you give them some of your time. These same kids are now grown, and when I see them, they usually remind me of some small activity we did together, like playing basketball. It may not have been a big act or gesture, but years later, as adults, they still remember the little things! Some of these grown children are now serving God and invite me to preach at their missions conferences!

Don't neglect the little things! Do them well and the opportunities to do bigger things will come. God will take note of your character and will entrust you with greater blessings in the future.

When something must be done, do it promptly. Attend to pressing matters immediately. The longer you wait, the more prone you will be to neglect the task. You may miss great blessings or experience great burdens if you fail to handle the small things promptly.

For loss of a nail, a horseshoe was lost. For loss of a shoe, a horse was lost. For loss of a horse, a soldier was lost. For loss of a soldier, a battle was lost. For loss of a battle, a war was lost. The war was lost because of the loss of a nail.

Neglecting the little things can cause a chain reaction that brings great dishonor to God.

When there is something to be done, do it pleasantly. The Lord wants us to serve Him with the right spirit. Don't complain that the task before you seems insignificant. Can you imagine what the church would be like if all the small chores were neglected or overlooked? What would the auditorium look like if the women of the cleaning ministry did not show up on Monday mornings? How would the grounds look without the faithful gardeners planting, watering, and trimming? How many soulwinning opportunities would be missed if there was no one to answer the church phone when someone needing spiritual guidance was desperately seeking help? Think about the children in the nursery running around unsupervised because not all the nursery workers showed up! Determine to serve the Lord with a pleasant and joyful spirit!

When there's a job to be done, do it with persistence. One of the secrets of a victorious Christian life is praying and reading God's Word persistently. We have to exercise our faith persistently. Keep doing the right things. Continue doing the small things well.

I had the privilege of taking Dr. Lee Roberson to lunch a few years ago. This great man of God has always kept such a busy schedule. I realized, as he shared some of his activities with me, that he does things *routinely*. Some of our responsibilities may seem mundane to us, but the more we keep at them, the better we get at performing them.

Dr. John Goetsch, Executive Vice President of West Coast Baptist College, is a man of discipline. He devotes time every day to run several miles. He gets up early each morning to have his time with the Lord and to memorize Scripture. If you have had the privilege of listening to him preach, you would know that he quotes many portions of Scripture from memory. His remarkable ability to memorize Bible verses is a result of setting aside time for study. Bible memorization requires hours of repetition, and Dr. Goetsch has learned to master these small disciplines. He is being used of God in a marvelous way, as a result.

Do the small things passionately. Develop a heart that loves to accomplish the things that need to be done. Every task you perform should be for the Lord, not for yourself or another person. Remember that God is in charge, so He won't give you a job that is too hard or that you cannot handle.

I like to do things with enthusiasm and with cheer. I realize that many of life's duties are monotonous, but the Lord enables me to do things cheerfully, as I stay surrendered to Him.

Do the little things prayerfully. The Apostle Paul says we are to pray without ceasing. It's so much easier to get things done when we have the right perspective, and that right perspective comes from a continual fellowship with God.

Perform the "insignificant" tasks patiently. Don't grieve the Holy Spirit by murmuring and complaining that you have the smallest responsibility in the church. Be thankful that you get to do *something* for the Lord. Do it with patience and with all your heart as unto the King of kings!

As large as the ministry is at Lancaster Baptist Church, its success is a result of people doing small things consistently well and always for God's glory. A good example of this would be the Easter and Christmas musicals presented for the community each year. There must be about four hundred people involved in those musicals. The fabulous productions are the result of hundreds of people collectively doing small tasks well.

All that is required for some people is to simply walk across the stage, and yet it contributes to the effectiveness of the drama. The entire production is composed of men in charge of sound, lights, props, and makeup. Several individuals form the drama team, orchestra, and choir. Behind the scenes are the nursery workers taking care of the children, so moms and dads can be at practices. The parking attendants, ushers, and greeters contribute by performing their duties. The music director ultimately depends on each person being in his place and doing his job well!

Is an action as small as shining your shoes important? It was a duty that I constantly performed until it became a habit. As an ambassador of Christ, it is important to look neat and well-groomed. Shined shoes is a small thing, but it can speak volumes to an unsaved person. How significant, then, is it to keep your car or your room clean? People can tell what kind of person you are just by looking at your car, house, or room. Do you have a passion for doing the small things in a great way?

Don't wait for an opportunity to do something great. Don't stand on the sidelines waiting for the big jobs to come along. Do the little things to the best of your ability day by day. Opportunities to serve the Lord in a greater capacity will come as you give your best effort to the little things that honor God.

PRINCIPLE SIX:
If I am careful to do the little things well, the big things will take care of themselves.

Whatsoever thy hand findeth to do, do it with thy might; for there is no work, nor device, nor knowledge, nor wisdom, in the grave, whither thou goest.
—ECCLESIASTES 9:10

PRINCIPLE SEVEN:

CHANGE IS ALWAYS POSSIBLE. NEITHER SUCCESS NOR FAILURE IS FINAL.

*Wherefore let him that thinketh he
standeth take heed lest he fall.*
—1 CORINTHIANS 10:12

7

CHANGE IS ALWAYS POSSIBLE. NEITHER SUCCESS NOR FAILURE IS FINAL.

Have you ever found yourself in what you thought was an impossible situation? God seems to specialize in leading His people into humanly impossible circumstances, and oftentimes, our first response is one of frustration or even hopelessness. Imagine how Moses felt with the armies of Pharaoh behind him and the Red Sea before him! Imagine how the disciples must have felt after Jesus sent them straight into a storm! Imagine how Joseph may have felt as God allowed him to be sold into slavery and then thrown into prison.

During times like these, we are tempted to throw up our hands in despair, but if you've walked with God for any length of time, you know that this is when God does His best work! This is when faith matters and God steps in.

So, what makes the difference? What makes change possible? **First, pray.** Prayer changes things! Taking impossible situations to God always sheds new light and perspective on any stage of life's journey.

Second, seek God and meditate on His Word. When you open the Bible, impossible and frustrating situations become opportunities for God to do something great.

Third, godly counsel encourages change and growth. Often, the faith of godly friends can help you see clearly when you feel that you're "up against a wall" spiritually.

God does many things that we cannot comprehend. He is God, and we have no right to question Him. The Lord says in Isaiah 55:8–9, *"For my thoughts are not your thoughts, neither are your ways my ways, saith the LORD. For as the heavens are higher than the earth, so are my ways higher than your ways, and my thoughts than your thoughts."*

It's easy to fall into a fatalistic mindset that our circumstances will never change. Sometimes, because we've been in a situation for five or ten years, we think that things will never get any better. It is easy to believe that we are permanently stuck in an unpleasant situation. We become afraid of remaining in an unfulfilling job, contending with the same troublesome people, or dealing with family problems that seem to never go away. We grumble that our spouse will never change, our children will never change, and the mission field will never change. Bear in mind that change is *always* possible with God!

You are on a journey with God, and He is always at work! Nothing about your life is static. God constantly desires to take you somewhere.

In the book of Esther, Haman, the prime minister under King Ahasuerus, plotted to kill the Jews. He hated Mordecai, Esther's cousin, who raised her like his own daughter after the death of her parents. He was able to convince the king that the Jewish nation was a bad lot. He made a decree that all the Jews were to be murdered in one day.

Haman even prepared gallows for Mordecai to be hanged. Esther 5:14 says, "*Then said Zeresh his wife and all his friends unto him, Let a gallows be made of fifty cubits high, and to morrow speak thou unto the king that Mordecai may be hanged thereon: then go thou in merrily with the king unto the banquet. And the thing pleased Haman; and he caused the gallows to be made.*"

When you read chapters 6 and 7, you find Esther interceding for her people, and it is Haman who ends up being hanged on the gallows! Esther exposed Haman's sinister plot, while the king granted the Jews the liberty to defend themselves and annihilate their enemies.

The point of the story is that no matter how bleak our circumstances are, change is always possible. In this instance, change was brought about overnight. Sometimes, it will take more than a day, or even more than a year, before we see the light at the end of the tunnel, but in God's plan, there is always hope at the end of struggle!

Many times, people who are caught in a difficult situation make very unwise decisions. They make decisions that could potentially ruin their lives and the lives of others. They *react* rather than *respond*. They jump ship rather than call out to God for divine intervention.

I sometimes ask myself, "Why is it that people focus on one bad thing when there are so many good things happening in their lives?" There may be one hundred good people encouraging and helping us, but we focus on the one person who gives us problems. There may be one hundred obvious blessings in our lives, but the one trial we face often gets most of our attention.

When I find myself in a difficult or trying circumstance, the best thing I can do is focus my attention on the Lord and concentrate on what He would have me to do. The answers to my problems can always be found in the Bible.

Over the years, my wife and I have found ourselves in many impossible situations. We have faced dozens of difficult trials and spiritual battles. In every one, we had to make a choice: either to focus on the impossibility of the problem or to focus on the power of God. When we focused on the problem, it only became bigger. When we focused on God, the problem became smaller. God always led and directed our steps.

When faced with the impossible, ask yourself these questions: Am I where God wants me to be today? Am I doing what God wants me to do? Am I doing the best I can to handle this situation?

If I can answer these three questions with a clear conscience and a pure heart, then I can rest assured that it's all in the Lord's hands.

I have often made this personal assessment: Maybe the *situation* is not the problem; maybe *I* am the problem. Perhaps the situation arose because there were things that I should have been doing but did not. Are there changes I should be making? Am I willing to change in order to improve my circumstance? Am I willing to make adjustments in my own life to better a relationship?

This same principle is true with success. Just as we tend to look at past struggles or failures and become frustrated, we also have the tendency to look at past successes and rest upon them.

Thank God for spiritual victories and past successes in your life. Don't ever get over them, and don't ever forget them. At the same time, however, don't stop pressing forward for God today just because you had a mountaintop experience yesterday!

Change is always possible. Having a good start in ministry is no guarantee for having a good end. Starting strong in a marriage is no guarantee of a life-long love. Just because things are going well in some area of your life doesn't mean you can drop your guard and coast for a while.

Regardless of the failure or the success, change is always possible. Don't get too high when things are going well. Don't get too depressed when things are going badly. Remember that neither success nor failure is permanent.

Ecclesiastes 11:4–5 says, "*He that observeth the wind shall not sow; and he that regardeth the clouds shall not reap. As thou knowest not what is the way of the spirit, nor how the bones do grow in the womb of her that is with child: even so thou knowest not the works of God who maketh all.*" If you do not sow, you will not reap. If you are content to sit idly and if you refuse to work because of wind or rain, you will not reap.

If you desire to reap change in your life, involve yourself in pursuits that will mature you in the Lord. Leave everything in His hands, and trust Him to produce the desired results.

PRINCIPLE SEVEN:
Change is always possible.
Neither success nor failure is final.

Wherefore let him that thinketh he standeth
take heed lest he fall.
—1 CORINTHIANS 10:12

PRINCIPLE EIGHT:

I MUST NOT TAKE MYSELF TOO SERIOUSLY.

For I say, through the grace given unto me, to every man that is among you, not to think of himself more highly than he ought to think; but to think soberly, according as God hath dealt to every man the measure of faith.
—ROMANS 12:3

8

I MUST NOT TAKE MYSELF TOO SERIOUSLY.

My dad often said concerning certain people: "If I could buy that man for what he's worth and sell him for what he thinks he's worth, then I'd be making a lot of money."

The Apostle Paul warns us against this type of pious thinking in Romans 12:3, "*For I say, through the grace given unto me, to every man that is among you, not to think of himself more highly than he ought to think; but to think soberly, according as God hath dealt to every man the measure of faith.*"

James 4:14 says, "*Whereas ye know not what shall be on the morrow. For what is your life? It is even a vapour, that appeareth for a little time, and then vanisheth away.*" Our lives are but a vapor. We are only here for a short time. Life is uncertain, but death is sure.

When my mother-in-law celebrated her one hundredth birthday, I interviewed her for a video we were producing on her life. She testified that she didn't feel like she was one hundred years old! (There weren't too many people around for her to ask how it was supposed to feel at one hundred!)

One hundred years didn't seem that long to her. (On a side note, always be careful how you treat your mother-in-law. She could be around a long time!)

In reality, life is short. When we compare our lives to eternity, they are but a drop in the bucket. We have not been here long; we will not be here long. God and the world existed without us for a long time, and they will manage without us after we're gone. It is unwise to consider ourselves so important that the world wouldn't be able to survive without us.

As servants of God, I believe we tend to overrate ourselves—to think more highly of ourselves than we ought to think. We take ourselves and our God-given roles too seriously. This not only dishonors God, it greatly limits what He desires to do in and through us. God will not share His glory, and when we exaggerate our supposed goodness, we are robbing God of His glory and exalting ourselves.

Please don't misunderstand. We need to be serious about the work of God. God has given all of us something to do, and we should take those responsibilities very seriously. We should take the ministry that He has given us seriously. The Apostle Paul said in Romans 11:13, "*I magnify mine office.*" Paul exalted his ministry, not himself. Regardless of what ministry the Lord has entrusted to you, do your very best to magnify that ministry rather than yourself.

We should not consider ourselves indispensable. It would not be right to think, "Without me, everything will fall apart." Only God is indispensable.

In the same way, we ought not to think that our opinion is indisputable. Don't come to a place where you think no one has a right to question you. Realize that others are there to help you and that your word is not the final word. Only God's Word is final.

Don't develop a "Messiah complex." It's not your job to save the world. Jesus is the only Messiah, and you are His servant. Adopt the attitude of John the Baptist when he said, *"He must increase, but I must decrease"* (John 3:30). When someone gets a Messiah complex, he feels he is indispensable. He thinks that without him, the work won't get done. He is the final authority on everything. We are but a voice crying in the wilderness. We are not even worthy to undo our Saviour's shoelaces.

Also, do not defend your mistakes. Do your best to correct them. When you blunder, admit it, instead of trying to cover it.

As parents, we might think that our children won't respect us if we admit our mistakes. Teachers may think their students will form poor opinions of them when they admit their mistakes. Preachers could think that the church members will not appreciate them if they admit their mistakes. Just the opposite is true! If there is anything that would build us up in the eyes of others, it would be when we confess that we've erred. After all, we all know that no one is perfect. No one is infallible, save the Lord Jesus Christ.

When you are willing to humble yourself, admit your mistakes, and defer the credit to others and the glory to God, you are making yourself a valuable vessel in God's hands. There is no telling how greatly God will use a heart with that spirit!

There have been times when after I've preached, Virginia has asked about something I said. My response is often, "I didn't say that." We'd take out the cassette tape, play it back, and, yes, there was the proof that she was right! I did say it! Hearing the cassette recording was proof of my mistake, even though I didn't want to admit it!

Others will respect you when they see you humbly admit to a mistake. Acts 15:36–41 tells us how the Apostle Paul and Barnabas had a dispute over whether or not they should take John Mark with them on their second missionary journey. Paul didn't think it was a good idea. Verse 39 says that their *"contention was so sharp"* that they had to part ways. Barnabas took John Mark with him, while Paul took Silas; however, in 2 Timothy 4:11, Paul mentioned how John Mark was *"profitable to me for the ministry."* Paul admitted that he had made an error in judgment.

Another way to avoid taking ourselves too seriously is to take time to "smell the roses." Enjoy the work that God is accomplishing in and around you. Enjoy the job

God has given you. The journey is just as interesting and exciting as the destination!

If we take ourselves too seriously, we will fail to set aside time to enjoy the blessings of God. I have good news for you: The world will continue moving forward if you take time with your family or if you take time to rest. Your ministry will do just fine if you take a day off. God has it all under control. He created you as a limited resource. Accept those limitations and let God be sovereign. Don't feel guilty to take some leisure time. We all need that once in a while, and you'll probably be a better Christian and servant of God because of it!

When our family was still living in Gary, Indiana, we planned to go to Chattanooga, Tennessee for a vacation. Virginia and I were very young, and Renee was only about a year old. We climbed into our '51 Pontiac and headed south. We wanted to visit Lookout Mountain and Ruby Falls. (Of course, at that time, we had no clue that the Lord would lead us to live in Chattanooga years down the road.) I must tell you that the fun began as soon as we started on the journey! It was more about spending time together and being together than it was about the destinations.

Oftentimes, regardless of where we're going on vacation, we think the fun starts when we get to our destination, but if we take the time to smell the roses along the way, our trips are more enjoyable.

You are on a journey in your life. Enjoy the simple pleasures God has given you.

I like to play golf. When I have the time, I play a round of golf with friends. If you have a hobby, do it. Don't feel guilty about taking time for something you enjoy. Take your spouse for a walk. Watch the sun set. Read a good book in front of a fire on cold days. God wants us to delight in the good things He has blessed us with.

Develop an outside interest, but don't let it consume you. Regardless of your regular job or line of work, you need to "get away from it all" every once in a while. Golf is a diversion for me. Some people like to fish, some like to hunt. Women like to shop, while some like to knit or crochet. There is nothing wrong with doing these things, as long as they don't become an obsession. Allow these recreational activities to be the seasoning of your life, not the main course. Let them renew your strength, restore your soul, and make you a better servant of the Lord. Even Jesus told His disciples to come apart for a season.

This principle often reminds me of a time I was in Asheville, North Carolina, during October for a missions conference. It was that time of year when the leaves were turning colors, and it looked like an artist had painted every imaginable color on the trees.

There is a place between Knoxville, Tennessee, and Asheville, North Carolina, that is unbelievably beautiful in the fall. I pulled over and just sat there for about thirty minutes—rejoicing and basking in the beauty of the Lord's creation.

Virginia and I seldom plan long vacations, but we do try to get away for a few days between meetings. Just recently, we were able to "sneak in" a two-day trip to an Amish country in Ohio. We had a wonderful time enjoying the goodness of God together. Delight in the places that God allows you to visit and the various pleasures He allows you to enjoy.

The Apostle Paul, after all the difficulties and trials he had been through, was able to say in the end, *"I thank Christ Jesus our Lord, who hath enabled me, for that he counted me faithful, putting me into the ministry"* (1 Timothy 1:12). Paul had every problem in the world, but he had the joy of knowing he did everything that God wanted him to do.

Friend, you're not the Saviour of the world. Jesus is. Serve Him, and enjoy the journey.

Principle Eight:
*I must not take myself
too seriously.*

*For I say, through the grace given
unto me, to every man that is among
you, not to think of himself more highly
than he ought to think; but to think soberly,
according as God hath dealt to every man
the measure of faith.*
—Romans 12:3

PRINCIPLE NINE:

EVERYONE AND EVERYTHING ARE MY TEACHERS. WE ARE INTERDEPENDENT.

For as the body is one, and hath many members, and all the members of that one body, being many, are one body: so also is Christ.
—1 CORINTHIANS 12:12

9

EVERYONE AND EVERYTHING ARE MY TEACHERS. WE ARE INTERDEPENDENT.

The verse I have claimed for this principle is 1 Corinthians 12:12, "*For as the body is one, and hath many members, and all the members of that one body, being many, are one body: so also is Christ.*" In this chapter, the Apostle Paul gives an analogy of the church and the physical body.

What does the word *independent* mean? As independent Baptists, we are autonomous as a local church. We are not under the authority of a fellowship. We're not ruled by any ecclesiastical body. We are not controlled by a denomination. In this case, we are independent.

This independence, however does not exclude our need for other people. We are independent Baptists, but as Christians, we are also interdependent. The Bible is very clear on the fact that we need one another.

I came upon this principle gradually. I didn't learn it in a day, but it struck a chord in my heart when I attended a seminar on the body of Christ (1 Corinthians 12) in Atlanta, Georgia. We had three sessions in the morning, three sessions in the afternoon, and a couple more in the evening. When I left the meeting that day, I left with a realization that I wasn't required to do everything by myself. God has designated different people to accomplish different jobs, but each person must work together for the cause of Christ to go forward.

I've preached in over one thousand churches during my years in ministry, and I can honestly say that I've learned something new in each church. Every pastor I have met has taught me some valuable lesson. I've learned lessons from my own students. I've never heard a sermon in which I did not learn something. We ought to make a commitment to glean from everything and everyone. We can even learn from someone else's mistakes, not just from our own!

Lancaster Baptist Church is an independent Baptist church, but we work with hundreds of other independent Baptist churches. A good example of working together for the cause of Christ is our missions program. One church giving one hundred dollars a month to support a missionary would not be sufficient for his ministry, but several churches individually giving the same missionary one hundred dollars a month, would enable him to get the job done.

First Corinthians 12 teaches us that the body has many diversified members. Verses 4–6 state, "*Now there are diversities of gifts, but the same Spirit. And there are differences of administrations, but the same Lord. And there are diversities of operations, but it is the same God which worketh all in all."* Verses 14–18 stress the significance of each member: *"For the body is not one member, but many. If the foot shall say, Because I am not the hand, I am not of the body; is it therefore not of the body? And if the ear shall say, Because I am not the eye, I am not of the body; is it therefore not of the body? If the whole body were an eye, where were the hearing? If the whole were hearing, where were the smelling? But now hath God set the members every one of them in the body, as it hath pleased him."*

God did not make us different so we could argue and quarrel. He intended for us to be interdependent. The following are comforting lessons I've learned about the body of Christ.

First, there is *something* I can do for the Lord. There are no insignificant or unimportant members in the body of Christ. You know this to be true in your own physical body. Even the members you don't see, play a role in keeping your body alive and healthy. Our internal organs work in harmony with each other to keep our bodies going. Even when one tiny part is hurting, the whole body suffers.

Second, I do not have to do *everything*. Can you imagine if the eye grumbled and said it was tired of seeing? Perhaps he wanted to be the ear for a day! That would definitely wreak havoc on the body, wouldn't it? If the ear decided to stop hearing and took the place of the nose, the body would go crazy! Even so, every member of the body of Christ has his or her own responsibility. God has chosen and set the members in the body to please Him. I may not always *understand* what the others in the church are doing, but I can certainly *appreciate* what they do to advance the work of the Lord.

I took a course several years ago from a renowned seminary teacher who said, "I don't understand it, but sometimes God blesses people who don't agree with me."

You will often find yourself not agreeing with another person, but realize that regardless of the way you feel, God can still bless and use that person. Let's face it, it's only by His grace that God can use *any* of us! God uses all of us *in spite* of ourselves, not *because* of ourselves! I am often amazed at what God does with me when I think of what He has to work through to accomplish it. I stand in awe over the fact that God could ever use me.

God has given to each of us a distinct personality, spiritual gifts, and specific resources. It is not my business to look behind my shoulder to inspect and worry about what others are doing. My responsibility is to use the spiritual gifts that God has given me to build up others.

God's work will be done by His Spirit. We're powerless to do anything without Him. It's not by power, nor by might, but by His Spirit that His work is accomplished.

I was preaching at an ordination service, when a young seminary student was asked if he was going to finish his education. I told this young man, "Jim, if you ever *finish* your education, quit preaching." I was trying to communicate to this young man that as long as we're alive, we should always be learning! Our education must continually be a work in progress.

I have tremendous respect for Dr. Paul Chappell, pastor of Lancaster Baptist Church. He is thirty years younger than I am, but he has been my teacher all the years that I have known him. He is a man of vision and integrity. He knows where he is going and how to get there. It's wonderful to work for someone like him. He's a man who loves the Lord, His Word, his wife and family, and God's people. I have observed him in all areas of the ministry at Lancaster Baptist Church. When God moves him to do something, he doesn't quit until the job is done.

As gifted as he is, he has remained humble. It's obvious to me that he does everything with others' spiritual growth and best interests in mind. He has a heart for people and a relentless passion for the lost. I would never have joined Lancaster Baptist Church if I thought for a moment that he was doing all this for himself.

There is a lesson to be learned in every situation and circumstance that arises in your life. There is something to be discovered from every person you meet. The question is: Will you open your eyes to the learning process around you?

Ask the Holy Spirit to enlighten your spiritual eyes. Determine to profit from the good, rather than point out the negative. Decide that you will learn from everyone and everything.

Let God be your teacher through every circumstance of your life, and from this moment until the Lord takes you home, don't ever stop learning!

PRINCIPLE NINE:
Everyone and everything are my teachers.
We are interdependent.

For as the body is one, and hath
many members, and all the members
of that one body, being many, are
one body: so also is Christ.
—1 CORINTHIANS 12:12

PRINCIPLE TEN:

BE ALL THAT YOU ARE
WHEREVER YOU ARE.

Whatsoever thy hand findeth to do, do it with thy might; for there is no work, nor device, nor knowledge, nor wisdom, in the grave, whither thou goest.
—ECCLESIASTES 9:10

10

BE ALL THAT YOU ARE
WHEREVER YOU ARE.

Jim Elliot was one of five young men killed on the beach in Ecuador by Auca Indians. His story is one of the greatest missionary stories of our generation.

I read in the book, *Through Gates of Splendor*, that he had written this principle on a page in one of his Bibles: "Regardless of where God puts you, be the very best you can be." First Peter 4:7 admonishes, "*But the end of all things is at hand: be ye therefore sober, and watch unto prayer.*"

We have no guarantee of tomorrow. We could die at any moment, or Jesus could return at any moment. We should treat each day as if it were our last. We should perform every task as if it were our last opportunity. Why? Because one day it will be.

We have a tendency to spend a lot of energy wishing we were somewhere else or wishing we were at a different stage of life. Choose to be content where God has placed you. If you're a child, enjoy being a child. If you're a teenager or adult, be all you can be for the glory of God.

If you're a senior saint, thank the Lord. You can teach the younger generation how to walk with God.

In Philippians 4:11 Paul asserts, "*Not that I speak in respect of want: for I have learned, in whatsoever state I am, therewith to be content.*" Contentment is not inherent in us. If you think it's innate, just watch children on the playground! It's the nature of the flesh to never be satisfied. Learning to be content is a lifelong process.

The Bible says in Isaiah 55:1–2, "*Ho, every one that thirsteth, come ye to the waters, and he that hath no money; come ye, buy, and eat; yea, come, buy wine and milk without money and without price. Wherefore do ye spend money for that which is not bread? and your labour for that which satisfieth not? hearken diligently unto me, and eat ye that which is good, and let your soul delight itself in fatness.*"

Why has the world gone crazy buying "things" to bring contentment and happiness to their lives? Contentment is not found in a place or in a person; it is found in the will of God.

Be content where God has placed you. Contentment does not lie in location. My wife and I have lived in Kentucky, Indiana, Illinois, Tennessee, Japan, and California. Considering all the places we've lived throughout our years in ministry, people often ask me which one I liked the best. It is impossible to choose which one we like best, because we have thoroughly enjoyed them all! In every place that God has allowed us to minister, we have fully experienced His blessings in our lives. Honestly, it doesn't matter where I live, as long as I'm sure God wants me in that particular place at that particular time!

We decided to make every place "home." We've not gone through life wishing we were at home; we've been at home in every place that God has led us. Learn to be content wherever God puts you.

Be content with the person or people with whom God put you. You've heard the saying, "It's hard to soar like eagles when you're working with turkeys." It's easy to blame others when things are not going our way, but Romans 12:16–18 states, "*Be of the same mind one toward another. Mind not high things, but condescend to men of low estate. Be not wise in your own conceits. Recompense to no man evil for evil. Provide things honest in the sight of all men. If it be possible, as much as lieth in you, live peaceably with all men.*"

Paul is teaching that even if some folks are almost impossible to deal with, we are still to display the right attitude of contentment.

I heard about a fellow sitting by another man on an airplane. They were engaged in small talk. The first man noticed that the other had his wedding ring on his right hand instead of his left. Curious, he asked, "Sir, I don't know whether I should ask this, but I noticed that you're wearing your wedding ring on the wrong hand. Is there a reason for that?" The other man answered, "Yes, I married the wrong woman!"

If you're married, you're not married to the wrong person! Contentment is not found in a person or a place, it's found in Jesus Christ.

Be content with what God gives you. This is probably the most difficult lesson to grasp in this day and age. Our nation has been blessed with abundant resources. We have so much, yet if we are not careful, the world will entice us to obtain more than we can afford or to covet things that God did not intend for us to have.

I read sometime ago that the average college student graduates with an average debt of thirty thousand dollars from student loans. Many people cannot go where God wants them to go in life and ministry, because they are so far in debt. They can't afford to leave their jobs! Many cannot give generously to the work of the Lord because they are saddled with a huge debt, as well. It is a sad thing to be in bondage to people because of debt.

Credit cards are not bad if you know how to use them. Pay them off completely each month or cut them up! The interest paid on credit cards is atrocious. It ought to be illegal to charge that much interest! Paying that interest is poor stewardship of God's blessings.

Years ago, I knew a missionary who had to leave the mission field, because he had accumulated over eighty thousand dollars in credit card bills. It's very easy to incur debt like this. We get an invitation in the mail almost daily from credit card companies offering us a "better deal" in terms of lower interest rates and finance charges.

There is nothing wrong with enjoying the financial blessings that God bestows upon us; however, we are not to be in ministry for financial gain. A big paycheck should not be our impetus in deciding which church to serve or where to go for God. Paul, in his epistles, mentions working with his hands to support himself in the ministry.

Matthew 6:33 says, "*But seek ye first the kingdom of God, and his righteousness; and all these things shall be added unto you.*" In other words, if you take God seriously and put Him first in your life, He'll bless you and provide for your every need.

The cure for poor stewardship is to be content with what God gives you. Trusting God and being content with Him alone does not mean you will be poor and miserable. On the contrary, God will give you more than you expect if you're faithful with the little you have now.

Paul, in his letter to the church at Philippi, thanked them for their offering: "*But I rejoiced in the Lord greatly, that now at the last your care of me hath flourished again; wherein ye were also careful, but ye lacked opportunity*" (Philippians 4:10). He continues his letter, "*I know both how to be abased, and I know how to abound: every where and in all things I am instructed both to be full and to be hungry, both to abound and to suffer need. I can do all things through Christ which strengtheneth me*" (Philippians 4:12–13).

Paul was determined to live on what God had provided for him. Life does not hinge on the abundance of things we possess.

I decided to not go into debt to fulfill a want, but I still occasionally have a want! I like good cars. Several years ago, I had a nice Buick Riviera. A friend of mine got into the car and was genuinely impressed by the leather seats and the power windows. He said to me, "I think I'll be a missionary, so I can get a car like this." That statement caused me to remember a time when Virginia and I, together with our two children, had to climb a hill to our house with our arms full of groceries, because we didn't have a car and didn't have the money for a taxi.

No one, at that time, expressed an interest in being a missionary, so he or she could go up and down the hill carrying groceries. It's easy to admire someone else's blessings without knowing their burdens or without understanding why God chose to provide.

From the bottom of my heart, if the Lord should decide to take away my car or my house, I wouldn't get angry with God. It would not disturb my contentment. If God gives me good things, I will enjoy them. If I have nothing, I will still enjoy God and my relationship with Him.

God is sovereign. He determines where you are and what you have. You determine what you will do with those circumstances and those provisions. You are the steward of these opportunities, and one day you will give an account to God for them. Don't bury them. Don't complain and gripe about what you don't have.

Choose to do the best you can with what God has placed into your hand. Learn to be content with who you are, what you have, where you are, and who you are with. Learn to be all that you can be right where God has placed you in life! He will bless you greatly as you strive to be all that you are wherever you are.

PRINCIPLE TEN:
*Be all that you are
wherever you are.*

*Whatsoever thy hand findeth to do, do
it with thy might; for there is no work,
nor device, nor knowledge, nor wisdom,
in the grave, whither thou goest.*
—ECCLESIASTES 9:10

CONCLUSION

CONCLUSION

There is no greater way to live your life than to base it upon the principles of God's Word. To God's glory and by His grace, Virginia and I have enjoyed fifty-three years of faithfully walking with God, serving Him together, and growing in His grace. Along the way, He has graciously taught us these principles, and He has greatly blessed them in our lives.

Too many Christians live by whim or emotion. They make decisions flippantly and fail to direct their lives by God's wisdom.

The Word of God is our most valuable resource for living. His truth stands firm, and His promises are trustworthy.

You will never regret charting the course of your life by the guiding principles of God's Word. You will never regret submitting completely to Him and surrendering your life to His will.

Thank you for taking time to read these ten principles. I hope and pray that God will instill them into your life, that you will review them frequently, and that you will pass them along to others. Let them anchor your life to God's plan and purpose.

Perhaps the hardest aspect of these ten principles is practicing them. Often, we know what is right to do, but we don't do it. May God grant you the courage, strength, and grace to live these principles. May you have the surrendered will to obey God.

Remember, He will honor you as you honor Him!

> *Blessed is the man that walketh not in the counsel of the ungodly, nor standeth in the way of sinners, nor sitteth in the seat of the scornful. But his delight is in the law of the LORD; and in his law doth he meditate day and night. And he shall be like a tree planted by the rivers of water, that bringeth forth his fruit in his season; his leaf also shall not wither; and whatsoever he doeth shall prosper. The ungodly are not so: but are like the chaff which the wind driveth away. Therefore the ungodly shall not stand in the judgment, nor sinners in the congregation of the righteous. For the LORD knoweth the way of the righteous: but the way of the ungodly shall perish.*—PSALM 1

May God greatly bless you as you seek to live your life based upon the guiding principles of His Word.

Other mini books available from Striving Together

These powerful little books make
perfect gifts of encouragement!

Done
by Cary Schmidt

Specifically created to be placed into the hands of an
unsaved person and a perfect gift for first-time church
visitors, this new mini book explains the Gospel in
crystal clear terms.

A Maze of Grace
by Dr. Paul Chappell

This mini book explores God's grace for His children
during a time of loss or trial. It's a great gift for hospital
visitation or for someone going through a storm.

What Is a Biblical Fundamentalist?
by Dr. Paul Chappell

Biblical fundamentalism is being redefined today. So,
what exactly is a biblical fundamentalist? In these pages
you will discover the history, the true definition, and
the clear-cut beliefs of someone who believes the basic,
central teachings of the Bible.

www.strivingtogether.com
800.201.7748

For more information about our ministry visit:

www.strivingtogether.com
for helpful Christian resources

www.dailyintheword.org
for an encouraging word each day

www.lancasterbaptist.org
for information about Lancaster Baptist Church

www.wcbc.edu
for information about West Coast Baptist College